HANDLING STOLEN GOODS

First published in Great Britain in 2019
as an Inscribe Chapbook
Peepal Tree Press Ltd
17 King's Avenue
Leeds LS6 1QS
UK

ISBN 13: 9781845234348

DEGNA STONE

HANDLING STOLEN GOODS

CONTENTS

STUPOR

The terrace on the other side of the park
catches the late sun in its windows
as the test match plays out on Jo's radio.

In the next room the wrong crowd inhale smoke,
fingers touching as the joint is passed around.

The day is hazy and the bloody paw prints
dragged in after last night's cat fight
are barely visible on the kitchen floor.

Kids with uniforms mangled by the day
drip through the park smoking tabs.

A car bleeding dub from its stereo
picks up the beat of my dehydrated brain.

It's too late to rewind seven weeks
and three days, or be someone else.

FOR LOVE

I replace poetry with a flawless
understanding of the offside law.
My voice becomes smoke, drifts
to the ceiling and swirls until
it sails through the door, joins the mist
that forms on the street around midnight.

It happens when we're stoned.
In fear of sounding stupid, I find
new ways to communicate, trace
words between your shoulder blades,
a language I can't speak. No one
notices the silence, that I've lost my tongue.

No one can tell us that we are too young.
We spend our time having sex and abortions.
Self-medicate anxiety, find shelter
in cynicism, exhaling smoke screens
that distract us from the wounds
we inflict on each other. I mouth words

that emerge as sounds without meaning.
Lost in a haze of hindu kush I listen to *Peel
Sessions* on a second-hand radiogram,
feel the jolt of P.J. Harvey singing *Sheela Na Gig.*
I shift the station through white noise,
trying to find an echo of my voice.

VÖRÐUR

The wind makes instruments of half-built tower blocks;
dissonant harmonics carve a path through my brain,
destroying its waymarkers until I can't find my way back.

The only peace is found in mountains echoing clouds,
so we leave the harbour but keep the coastline in view.
If we lose sight of it, we believe the sea will vanish.

The city shifts.
We find ourselves
at the ghost of the old shoreline,

where you tell me tales of houses that wander through town,
and statues that walk from overlooked corners to find a home,
where the swans protect us from nykur but not ourselves.

*

The wind grows fierce at Reykjanes.
We don't know where to begin so we wind
our way across the ash-black landscape.

The heather looks like embers,
sand grits between our toes.
We topple the waymarkers as we walk.

We aren't interested in finding our way back.
There is no point in going back.
We are not going home.

*

You sit away from the edge of the cliff in the lea of a waymarker.
I stand with my back to the sea watching you, willing the wind

to take the feet from under me and hurl me into the air.
I imagine myself floating down like Jesus descending from heaven,

submerging past monochromatic birds littering the swell,
freeing myself of the bond that ties me to the landscape.

But the wind dies down and here I still am,
still watching you sit in the lea of a waymarker.

*

Tell me stories of how the water baptised you,
took away your sense of self. How it will heal you,

or kill you. The ocean's will to let you escape
with your life depends on the moods of its tides.

What happens when the sea turns against you,
when it tires of the burden of you on its surface?

God's name won't leave your lips,
sticks in your throat and drowns the good in you.

*

We took our love at face value. Failed to see
the horror that was visible from behind.

Never knew the difference between falling
and falling in love.

We meet ourselves coming back from the edge
of our senses. Feel the emptiness more than ever.

How can I be responsible for your heart,
when I am no longer responsible for my own?

notes: Vörður – way markers, nykur – water demons that take the form of horses.

IN TOO DEEP

Knowing that we
were not what we wanted,
        we strayed

miles from anyone
who would care
        if we went in too far.

We pulled each other further in,
neck deep, the river bed
        slipshifting under our feet.

The water stripped our skin,
nerve ends shut down

        we were raw.

I waited for you to resurface,
looked back at the space
        where you should have been –

when they pulled
us out

        we were gone.

CROSS BONES BURIAL GROUND

(Since then, each night contains all others)

Dried up roses faded to brown,
a handmade Red Cross flag
tied between the square bars of the gate,

champagne corks, raffia bows –
whatever these Southwark mourners
had to hand to show they care.

It looks like the site of a stabbing
or an industrial accident,
another post-Diana shrine.

Coming back that way late one night,
caught up in a procession for *the outcast dead*
I learned its meaning.

I threaded the smooth silver key ring you left me
onto a piece of greyed-out red ribbon,
left your memory there.

A SPARK

i.m. Kenneth Arrowsmith Stone

…and it's like I'm floating
with the weight of the universe pressing
against every part of my body

and I long for the peace of an abandoned city
piled high with cubes of compressed rubbish
and the barest hint that human life could return…

I want to transform into an angular robot
with a naïve understanding of life and love,
who prefers the magic of a Zippo lighter to the fire

of a diamond ring, who follows his love across
the universe; recharges in the glare of the sun,
not needing to breathe.

Instead, on Earth, it feels like we've forgotten how to dance.
Your writing jitters like you'd been caught in a sandstorm:
"I think I am becoming unwell…"

We keep our heads down, remember the days
when blue skies were animated
with cartoon-perfect clouds,

forget that we haven't learned to repair ourselves
and no spark of electricity
can bring you back to who you were.

RED LIGHT

after Sean Scully

When the news leaves you feeling overshadowed,
leaves you living in the ruins of avoidable disasters,
you find sanctuary, find salvation, in the Laing.

Inside the gallery there is never total peace.
The air conditioning stage-whispers white noise,
the type that might soothe a fretful baby.

Standing in front of Red Light you want to scream,
want the red lines to absorb the pain ripping your throat,
hollowing your lungs. You want to be heard.

You shrink until the painting holds the menace
of a tower block, with all the horror that brings –
the thought of being trapped, being afraid to die.

To calm yourself, you count the colours, count the lines,
try to figure out which was laid down first.
You want to disappear into this painting.

At the lower right corner there is a luminescence.
The spaces between the lines seem bigger,
there's more room to think, more room to be yourself.

You wait until you are completely alone,
then cross the border of the painting,
picking your way under each stripe of acrylic,

challenging yourself to travel further in
until you reach the ground, the first layer of paint,
with its complexity of colour, its sinuous waves.

You still cannot find rest, your mind is too full
of where you have been, of what you have left behind.
You realise each red line links you to someone you've loved

even as these same red lines hold you hostage,
keep you caged inside the painting
with no way to get back through.

THE CROWS

are eating a carcass I won't recognise
as a fox cub until my car is almost upon it.

I'm not sure that they'll shift
but I've never seen a crow splattered

across the road, its brethren flying down
to peck at its remains burst open by traffic.

Maybe that's why they take their time,
why they're so bold. They can't die.

I want to be as black as the crows –
to grow my face as hard as theirs,

sharpen my beak on the bones
of the dead – be unafraid.

PERFIDIA

It's like listening to Siri navigate
after his voice changed in the update.

You know what he's saying
but not what he's getting at.

It's his diction. Clipped. Like
he's withholding something from you.

How can you trust him?
You want to see the shape of his mouth,

watch the words physically form
on the lips he doesn't have.

How can you understand what he's saying
if you can't see what he's saying?

Instead, his words appear by magic.
And who can understand magic?

GHOSTING

Last night I dreamt your daughters were dead
and you were dying. I don't know why,
though I think of you often and miss you all still.

My girls do too, when they allow themselves
to remember you. It's not something we talk about.
I've edited out our mutual friendships

and this is where we find ourselves now,
avoiding each other on the street,
meeting in dreams.

ALLOTMENT

We take old ice cream tubs from the shed,
wait to be shown which fruit to pick –
gooseberry, loganberry, blackcurrant.

A bass line of city traffic underscores
the hum of insects and bird chatter,
creates a song for me and my sister.

We listen to Mum and Dad pick over
last night's rows as they tease
out the bindweed creeping over the plot,

strangling this year's crops.
Mum watches us carry our harvest
to the stand pipe, rinse off dust and grubs;

our hands stop berries tumbling over the edge
as we pour sunlit water back into the earth.
We sit in the shade of the shed and eat.

SHOPLIFTING IN MERCIA

The Ankerside store detectives and I had become too familiar. We could see each other coming, or maybe it was that we were highly sensitised to each other's smell. The aisles of the shops held no sport for me now, so I made my way out into the Castle Grounds and indulged my kleptomania there. I took Æthelfæd's statue and pocketed it. Secreted the Kings of Mercia under my jacket, tucked them under my arms to stop them slipping loose. I coaxed The White Lady from the Tower, wrapped her around my leg and let her haunt my skirt. I took them all home, played hooky with them when I should have been at school.

HANDLING STOLEN GOODS

"If you lie to me, I'll tear your throat out."
Anansi's Tiger

Summer hasn't given up its heat.
Mum, already halfway up the stairs,
screams for me to come from my room.

Did you tell Anna?

We mustn't tell lies
but outside this house
the opposite is true.

Clarting around last week
in Anna's dusty backyard
the truth caught up with my tongue,

spilled the words into her ears.
No one had said why
I shouldn't tell anyone about

the VCRs in our house.
Turns out they were hooky –
Anna's dad is a policeman.

Did you tell her?

Mum's hands splay out
like a shadow-play dove,
flutter at my throat.

THE HOUSE THROWN OUT BY HER VILLAGE

The house thrown out by her village sits isolated in a patch of abandoned ground, her windows glaucomaed with grime. Her floors and ceilings have crumbled, taken away the definition of rooms. She is all space. If you can take the danger of not knowing where to put your feet she'll welcome you in with an open door. There is a lack. A missing. A want. She is breaking down, has broken down but despite being alone for so long she has not grown tired of herself. Listen hard and keep a sense of where everything used to be. And where your room could have been.

BEFRIENDING THE CROWS

for Theresa May

She wanted to understand something of herself but she didn't
have the answers, so she tried to befriend the crows. She liked
the way their feathers absorbed the sun, the way they radiate energy.
She was friendless and needed company, even the corvid kind.
She'd read a long time ago that they could be coaxed with gifts.

She started with the mouse she found dead at the foot of the stairs,
then tried fatballs made from vegetable suet and the seeds of flowers
she'd meant to plant in the spring. When fortune cookies with secret
messages she was sure they were smart enough to decipher failed,
she tried to coax them with a replica measure from the Jewel Tower

and an iron roof-plate that fell into the Thames from the Elizabeth Tower.
She tried a confusion of biddable politicians, miniaturised to pocket size,
and a brushful of her hair woven into love tokens. She wanted to offer up
the secret to life, the universe and everything, if she'd known it,
but suspected the crows already did and were keeping it to themselves.

She hoped the crows would be curious but worried that they would
worry about the sanity of her mind instead. Then when they came, or even
if they didn't, she'd tell them the things that were troubling her,
that this journey isn't worth the shoe leather, and where she's heading
feels like hell.

SHORT-SIGHTED

Men with spines as strong as the Tyne Bridge
are building flat-bottomed boats
too small to rescue even minuscule folk.

They seal the hulls with the green
that grows on top of yoghurt.
A fleet for known unknowns.

You can tell them the boats will take on water,
won't float – but you're wasting your breath;
they won't listen.

Go to your homes. Cup your worries
in your palms, turn them over and over
until they are cultured to pearls.

BLACKFACE

Live Theatre, Newcastle. 3 December 2017

It's the sucker punch of an actor walking onstage wearing blackface;
the roar from the audience as they piss themselves laughing.
Though the grease paint is wiped clean, there's an indelible stain.
The context has shifted but the old problems are the same.

OF MUTUALITY

Look down at your hand, the colour of your skin,
now imagine it was *other*, whatever *other* means.

Watch the pigment rise (or fade), feel the texture
of your hair change, blink the ache from eyes

refocusing in their new shade.
How does the world look now?

This happened in a flash but a pricking
sensation lingers. This is not an abstract,

and though it terrifies you, *in a real sense*
there is no going back.

You've been holding your breath; breathe out,
panic won't help. Find someone who looks like

you used to, let your lives intersect.
What will you do now, in your new skin?

MOTHER COUNTRY

i.m. The British West Indies Regiment

Any negro or person of colour, although an alien may voluntarily enlist
and when so enlisted, shall be deemed to be entitled
to all the privileges of a natural-born British subject.

Manual of Military Law 1914

She was not a loving mother.
Nurturing did not come easy.

Lucky he was raised to look up to her,
to respect her, trust her. *Mother knows best.*

She kept him out of sight, gave him the dirtiest chores,
never allowed him to play with others.

She didn't know how to give him what he needed,
thought her boy hardier than he turned out to be.

She should have wrapped him up warm,
but she let him shiver, almost catch his death.

When he fell ill she thought he was faking –
until his temperature reached 100 degrees

and vomit pooled around his feet.
Some people aren't cut out to be parents.

He didn't think she was cruel, he loved her.
He never complained, not at first.

His smile could reach around the earth
but couldn't penetrate her heart.

When she realised she could never love him
she wanted him gone, out of sight.

Ashamed of her failings she was quick
to pack his things into boxes,

to hand him over, send him back.

WORD OF MOUTH

When my parents spoke, something in my ear clicked
off and I never knew how to switch it back on.

I spoke to you in your mother tongue, you replied in mine.
But I remember that your speech was slightly off,

that even though you told me you were fluent,
in another language you are slightly someone else.

I'LL NEVER PROTEST AS WELL AS NINA SIMONE

If I could sit in a too hot bath
and let the water strip this anxiety
from my skin, I would.

I would sing protest songs
to myself. Keep the notes
inside my head.

I'd wonder how the science
behind layers of skin cells
translates into hatred,

how this water-resistant
membrane became
a barrier.

I thought I had made peace
with my skin, learned
to live within it

                    forgotten
its tone could make someone
feel sick to their stomach.

We cannot live outside our skin.
We are tied to it, shackled to it,
bound by it. Even you,

especially you.

BIOGRAPHY

Originally from the Midlands, Degna Stone is a poet, editor and producer based in Tyne & Wear. She is a co-founder and former managing editor of *Butcher's Dog* poetry magazine, and a contributing editor at *The Rialto*. She holds an MA in Creative Writing from Newcastle University and received a Northern Writers' Award in 2015. Degna is a fellow of The Complete Works III and received a Hawthornden Fellowship in January 2019.

ACKNOWLEDGEMENTS

"Stupor" was first published in *Lucifer* magazine. "Vörður" was commissioned for Waters and Harbours in the North, a partnership project between New Writing North, Writers' Centre West in Gothenburg, UNESCO City of Literature in Reykjavik and The Nordic House in Torshavn in the Faroe Islands. "Cross Bones Burial Ground" was first published in *Ten: Poets of the New Generation* (Bloodaxe) and the epigraph is taken from Michael Donaghy's poem "Black Ice and Rain". "A Spark" makes reference to the character Wall·e in the Disney Pixar film of the same name and was first published in *Double Bill* (Red Squirrel Press). "Red Light" was commissioned by Newcastle Poetry Festival in response to a major retrospective of work by Sean Scully. "Perfidia" and "The House Thrown Out by her Village" were first published in *Filigree: Contemporary Black British Poetry* (Peepal Tree Press). The epigraph for "Handling Stolen Goods" is taken from Neil Gaiman's version of the Anansi stories. "Befriending the Crows" contains a nod to Douglas Adams' "Life, the Universe and Everything". An earlier version of "Blackface" was published in *And Other Poems*. "Of Mutuality" was first published in *The Mighty Stream: Poems in Celebration of Martin Luther King* (Bloodaxe). "Mother Country" was commissioned by identity on tyne as part of *Presence*, a project that explored the presence of Black and Asian troops during the First World War.